MASTER YOUR MIND

By Louise Cowley

The Map

INTRODUCTION- THE IMAGINATION IS THE CREATIVE SOURCE	2
THE PRACTICAL	6
1. MEDITATE	6
2. VISUALIZE	7
3. LIVE IN THE END	10
THE THEORY	16
1- FAITH IS LOYALTY TO UNSEEN REALITY	16
2- OCCUPYING THE STATE	33
3. PERSIST IN THE ASSUMPTION	50
CONCLUSION-PERSEVERANCE	59
EXAMPLES OF CREATING CONSCIOUSLY FROM THE LECTURES OF NEVILLE GODDARD	66
EPILOGUE	91

INTRODUCTION- The Imagination IS the creative source

Man is all imagination and God is Man, and exists in us, and we in Him.
William Blake

The idea that the imagination is the source of all that appears in our world is not generally accepted by the more rationally minded among us. The very notion of it is likely to be met with some derision or awkward silence for the person who raised it. At the opposite extreme, it may be accepted without any examination of what this could actually mean. There are very few who can look at it intellectually and spiritually with an open mind. It is my hope that those who read this book will at least consider the empowering idea that our world is not created through external phenomena but purely through our imagination.

If we really want to gain an understanding of the imagination as the creative source, we need to study and contemplate spiritual insights with an open and questioning mind; not merely saying we understand this but actually living this truth from moment to moment.

Although, we may have revelations of the truth, we forget and put more faith in the facts of the world than the power that lives within us. This is not to deny the reality of the outer world of becoming, but to recognize that everything we see is a manifestation of the mental activity that goes on in our imagination. We need to make our belief into a way of life so that the power within us, is used naturally and often.

MASTER YOUR MIND

We create our world through our thoughts and our feelings, so isn't it time we learnt to master our mind? Imagine if we could harness the power within us to manifest positive situations for ourselves and others instead of allowing the mind to run wild with random, negative and self-destructive thoughts. Imagine how calm, serene and happy we could be. All it takes is the motivation to change and the desire to break old habits and practice the new. We need to use the mind as a tool of manifestation. Our goal is to imagine a new concept of self and we can start by asking ourselves the following questions:

How would you see yourself if you achieved what you want to achieve?
How would you feel?

When we can clearly imagine this feeling, we need to live in it throughout the day and this feeling will eventually appear in the world as objective reality. Everything already exists and the way to bring this into everyday life is through imagining the feeling of what it would be like; in other words, the feeling of the wish fulfilled. However, if we do not learn to master our mind, it will go off in many different directions and we will find ourselves far away from our dreams in time and space.

We can start by following a routine first thing in the morning and last thing at night before we fall asleep. Throughout the day, we can rest in the feeling of the wish fulfilled as often as we can. This will lead to a more balanced and fulfilling life where we are less disturbed by unpleasant situations, understanding the dreamlike nature of life. We will be more focused on what we cannot yet see but know beyond a shadow of a doubt, is a fact in 'the invisible'. Through our faith in its existence, it will appear when the time is right in the world of the senses.

Now is always the best time to make a new start and build a lasting routine that will change our lives for the better and allow us to fulfill our true potential.
Truth depends upon the intensity of the imagination- not upon facts.
-Neville Goddard

THE PRACTICAL

1. MEDITATE

In order to increase your awareness of the activity of your mind, begin with meditation. This will help you to notice negative thoughts and then you can exchange them for those of a more productive nature and the feeling of the wish fulfilled. Meditating will also increase your awareness of memories when you have imagined something, and it has appeared in your world thus developing your faith in how things appear.

Start the day by meditating on your breath. Even meditating for just ten minutes will show you how quickly your mind jumps from one random thought to another. Despite this, there is no need to lose hope that you will ever gain control over your mind. The key is simply to notice when you get lost in thoughts and return your focus to the breath. Sit upright in a chair or on a cushion and practice breathing in and out deeply and calmly. Essentially, you are practicing bringing your mind back to awareness and consequently to the feeling you would have, if you were to achieve your dream.

It is not necessary to close your eyes but it helps by shutting out the senses and removing attention from the physical reality of the material world. You can do this anywhere you are able to relax and turn inwards.

Rest in the feeling of simply being. Focus on the words, 'I AM' spoken quietly to yourself or within until you feel you are resting in the present moment. Relax into that state of peace.
Now you are in a relaxed and focused state, you are ready to visualize having what you want; then simply rest in the feeling this produces.

Learn to separate your identity from being the mind to being the master of the mind.

2. VISUALIZE

You can sit upright or lie down and either keep your eyes partially open or close them, but it is often easier to close them and shut out the senses.

What you want in life is often easier to answer than, 'Who do you want to be?' but the concept you hold of yourself is instrumental in whether you achieve your desire or you do not. To be successful, you have to see yourself as a success so when you know what you want, imagine how you would feel if you obtained it. What kind of person would you become? What kind of person do you want to be? See yourself through these eyes as though you were that person now.

Mentally construct a scene which implies that your desire is realized. It must FOLLOW how it is achieved- how everything falls into place is not your concern. There is no requirement from you to plan how to make it happen.

Create a short scene that implies your desire is fulfilled. Make it short, vivid, colorful and full of joy. Use all the senses and move in the scene. See people you know as being happy for you and seeing you differently after your success. Do not see yourself as though you were watching yourself in a movie, but as though you are part of the scene and seeing it through your own eyes.

You are the eyes seeing everything unfold around you as in life. Create a short piece of dialogue between yourself and someone you know, again, implying the desire is realized. Your friend could start the conversation with, 'I remember when...' e.g.- 'I remember when you were struggling with money, but now your life is completely different!' By using, 'I remember when...', there is an immediate implication that this time has passed, and your circumstances have changed. Continue the conversation expressing your joy and gratitude for your current situation. End this scene on a freeze frame with the single sensation of fulfilment dominating your mind. When you open your eyes, it should almost feel like a shock that you are not where you were in the imagination as it was so realistic and vivid as though you were actually there... and indeed, you were there.

When you merge yourself in the feeling of achieving your dream, you should feel a sense of fulfilment and gratitude to the power within you for bringing this into your life. Yield completely to this feeling and give thanks with words or silently, from within.

Revisit this scene regularly until it feels extremely vivid and the mind does not go off in a different direction. It is particularly beneficial if you can imagine the scene as you are falling asleep and take the feeling into the subconscious. You can also imagine you are sleeping in a different place- the place you might live if you fulfilled your dream.

3. LIVE IN THE END

When you imagine your dream, a particular feeling arises. During the day, carry that feeling around with you as though it were a fragrance you were wearing and believe that your imaginal act is a fact… because it is. You have entered into the state of how it would feel if you achieved your dream, the new concept of self. This is 'living in the end' where you move forward in time to the state you would experience if you became the person you want to be. Feeling must come first; the physical manifestation will follow if you persist in your assumption.

When you live in the feeling of the wish fulfilled, there is an assumption that it is done. Remind yourself of this frequently by using the words, 'I AM' followed by what you wish to be. Remain relaxed that you have what you want. You can also increase this relaxed feeling by telling yourself, 'It's a fact' until you believe it without question.

Always assume the best and forget the rest. Give objective reality a light touch and suspend judgement on anything that happens to you, knowing that you do not know how your dream will appear, but you know that it already exists in the imagination. Whatever happens, do not lose faith in the power of the imagination. It may well be that how situations manifest are a test to see if you can keep faith in your dream. Listening to talks by Neville Goddard, reading his books and contemplating key scripture are all ways you can maintain the view that your environment is part of you.

You need to see yourself as already being the person you want to be and move mentally from thinking <u>of</u> the end result, to thinking <u>from</u> the end result. As you are the new concept of self, think from this concept and new ideas will arise. It is like playing make-believe as a child and so have fun with it and your play will yield great results.

God is your own wonderful human imagination- the potter- which means 'the imagination' in Hebrew. The Bible speaks of God symbolically as the potter, molding different forms from the one piece of clay.

Truth depends upon the <u>intensity</u> of the imagination

A series of events will eventually unfold, leading up to the fulfilment of the state you are currently living in. Feed the mind with assertions presumed to be true using 'I AM', because assumptions though false, if persisted in until they have the feeling of reality, will eventually harden into fact. See the world from the view that you have achieved your dream and carry on inner conversations from this premise and the subconscious will eventually express this in waking reality.

It is important to not take objective reality too seriously and respond well rather than react to perceived negative events. You do not know how your desire will manifest and so try to suspend judgement and keep an open mind. Always notice your own negative thoughts and exchange them for positive thoughts concerning the wish fulfilled. This will become easier, and you will be able to drop negativity quickly knowing that it does not serve you and keeps you from happiness in the future and most certainly, in the present moment.

A negative thought can turn to a negative feeling in a moment. It could happen from a perceived slight which then might lead to a train of thoughts analyzing why one particular person does not like you when nothing may be further from the truth. Whatever has led up to the negative feeling, you can help to loosen it up by changing your perspective, focusing on the desired state and using positive affirmations.

Recall a positive memory regarding the person who has upset you and know that everyone you meet is fighting their own hard battle. Imagine how it would feel to become the person you want to be when you have fulfilled your dream and understand when you rest in that state, you are already there. The whole thing is done.

You can also remind yourself that this is simply objective reality, a shadow world and what you are experiencing may actually be adding to your future happiness in some strange way. These are just a few suggestions on how to loosen up negative feelings once they are there, but you will experience them less, the more you focus on positive thoughts and assume the best about people. Seeing others as friends and responding to them in this way will lead to a lot more goodwill and any perceived negativity will have less and less power over you. Imagine people's faces smiling at you and being friendly and this is what you will begin to experience in everyday reality.

It is important to emphasize that having temporary negative feelings will not have a detrimental effect on manifesting your dreams. It is not so much about constantly maintaining a certain feeling that manifests your desire, it is about <u>assuming it is already done</u>. Thinking that you must always be experiencing positive feelings will lead to a sense of failure and even fear of a certain outcome. It is normal and healthy as human beings to experience the full range of human emotions. What is negative is when we hold onto unpleasant feelings that bring us down. Learn to let go quickly so that you feel good again. You could also keep a book of manifestations to record successful outcomes. This will help to develop your faith.

So, train the mind to always choose positivity over negativity; it is not naivety, it is choosing happiness in the present moment.

Main Points

    1. Meditate
    2. Visualize
    3. Live in the End

Summary- Live in the feeling of the wish fulfilled

Training the mind

1. Visualize your desire first thing in the morning and last thing at night

2. Carry around the feeling of the wish fulfilled

3. Assume you already have what you want

THE THEORY

1- FAITH IS LOYALTY TO UNSEEN REALITY

Faith is the assurance of things hoped for, the evidence of things not seen.
Hebrews 11:1

By faith we understand that the world was created by the Word of God so that things which are seen were made out of things which do not appear. If you see it clearly, you will see that faith does not give reality to unseen things, it is loyalty to the unseen reality that gives meaning to the word 'faith'.

All things exist. Eternity exists and all things in eternity, independent of creation. So, on this level, the shadow level, we do not see the reality. We do not see the source, the cause of it all. That's where we are called upon to exercise faith- loyalty to unseen reality. It really is the abandonment of self. It is an act of self-commission and man cannot commit himself to what he does not love and scriptural faith is faith in God. So, any idea that we have a God which

does not spontaneously call forth out of our hearts the feeling of love, is not a true idea of God. For the whole basic matter is that God is love.
Faith is Loyalty to Unseen Reality (Lecture) - Neville Goddard

THE INTERNAL AND THE EXTERNAL

God gives us free will to believe either that all things are created externally or that all things come from within and that we are the operant power. If we believe that all things are created externally, we believe in a world of competition where there is a limited number of resources we must fight for. If we believe that everything already exists in the invisible as the Bible states, and that we only have to persevere in believing in its existence for it to eventually appear in our world, we believe in unlimited abundance for all. That choice demands spiritual understanding and faith in the word of God. We can deepen this understanding by studying the scripture that pertains to it. The word of God is alive, and it <u>will</u> yield results if you give yourself time to contemplate its deeper and more hidden meanings.

The alternative choice is to trust completely in the world which gives no reassurances or promises or indeed, permanent comfort. Instead, it offers a pervasive anxiety coupled with fear and doubt. We receive an unspoken message, said or believed, that we are not good enough and that there are many more who have a greater chance of achieving their dreams than we do. It is a world of competition with a poverty mentality where we must fight to succeed.

We are thrown at the mercy of circumstance, never knowing what is around the corner and hoping for the best but often fearing the worst. Worldly people may feel sensible and rational and perhaps look at others who believe in an invisible world as being at best, eccentric and at worst, crazy. All that produces is a cynical sense of superiority from time to time.

Is it really worth it?

Some will think that those who believe in creation from within, do so out of a need to feel control and for some people, this will be true. This however, does not mean that it is not the truth.

There is no need to announce your beliefs to everyone. There is no need to hide them either. It is not about what other people think, it is about what you are able to imagine.

In order to really develop your faith and your ability to use your imagination to manifest your dreams and desires, you must study and contemplate and meditate upon scripture. There is no other way. Having a superficial understanding of the process will not enable your faith in the invisible to stay strong when objective reality hits you hard. It is also no hardship to study scripture which feeds the soul and can bring great spiritual joy.

So, without further ado, choose to deepen your belief and understanding so that you are able to call all things into being through the power of the imagination.

THE SHADOW LEVEL

Our world can be called the shadow level as it contains the shadows of things previously imagined.

If you will but enter a state in your imagination, and assume its truth, the outer world will respond to your assumption, for it is your shadow, forever bearing witness to your inner imaginal activity.
-Neville Goddard 04-19-1969- ALL THAT YOU BEHOLD

Your outer world is built on your assumptions but the second man, the Lord from Heaven lives within us and is the supplanter. We can supplant old assumptions with new ones. However, it is sometimes hard to believe in our new imagined state when we are living on the shadow level and what we see reflected back to us is our old state.

All that you behold, though it appears without, it is within, of which this world of mortality is but a shadow.
William Blake

It can also be called the shadow level as we live in a world of death. Everything dies here- cut it and it bleeds- but the reality is that it is all illusion as there is no death. Consciousness is the only reality and we are consciousness. Know that a change in the shadow level will follow a change in consciousness. Believe in your assumption and it will eventually manifest in your world as everything always has, up until this present moment.

Everything already exists in the invisible. Your imagined state already exists- all you have to do is enter it, feel how it feels and believe that it exists. You can know it exists as you are feeling the state you have chosen to feel. What you feel IS the actual state. As you dwell in it, it starts to gain substance in a mysterious way and it will eventually appear in this world. All you have to do is persist in the belief and the belief will bring you the experiences. Everything already exists in the unseen and all we have to do is occupy the imagined state. It is faith in this, that will make the desired state manifest in the world.

Feeling the desired state should bring forth a feeling of joy and love as this is what you want more than anything. This is also merging with

your Creator who IS love. You give yourself up to him as you feel yourself into the desired state and thank him from within.
Yield to the being within, convinced that he heard you as He has.
How could He not, if he lives within?

SCRIPTURE TO CONTEMPLATE

In the beginning was the Word, and the Word was with God, and the Word was God. The same was in the beginning with God.
All things were made by him; and without him was not anything made that was made. In him was life; and the life was the light of men. And the light shineth in darkness; and the darkness comprehended it not.
- John 1: 1-5

Jesus is the Word of God. He is within us as the Divine Imagination and within him all things exist. We draw things out of this well of life through feeling how it would feel to be the person we want to be. There is no other way to bring things into your world than this way.

All things were made by him; and without him was not anything made that was made.
-John 1:3

There is not a single exception to this. To truly know this is to feel awe.

He was in the world, and though the world was made through Him, the world did not recognize Him.
-John 1:10

The world does not see its own creator. It does not see from whence He came. The source of His existence remains hidden to them. Many are so focused on the seeming duality of the world, they cannot comprehend that everything that appears to be external, began in the imagination… but it did.

For in Him all things were created, things in heaven and on earth, visible and invisible, whether thrones or dominions or rulers or authorities. All things were created through Him and for Him.
- Colossians 1:16

All things that exist in the invisible, exist in Him. He is the source of creation. Everything belongs to Him and exists because of Him and for Him. Why for Him? Could it be for the expansion of love?

By faith we understand that the universe was formed at God's command, so that what is seen was not made out of what was visible.
-Hebrews 11:3

If what is seen was not made out of what was visible, it was made from the invisible, the imagination. God commanded things to exist and they did. We also have this power as He lives within us.

But in these last days He has spoken to us by His Son, whom He appointed heir of all things, and through whom He made the universe.
-Hebrews 1:2

And God said, 'Let there be light, and there was light.
-Genesis 1:3

God spoke through the Word and all things were created. We can speak through the Word and manifest a new state of life.

FAITH

Many people would describe faith as belief but would stop right there and not really know how to implement it in a practical sense. They see it as an abstract concept in the same way they see God, and if pressed, may say it is believing that God will answer prayers. This is correct but if we are to be really clear and specific on what faith means, and how to use it in prayer, we are less likely to allow doubt into our thoughts which is poison to our dreams being fulfilled.

Now faith is the substance of things hoped for, the evidence of things not seen.
-Hebrews 11:1

Describing faith as a substance gives it a sense of being a material through which our dreams are created. It can be compared to the potter's clay that is reworked into another vessel.

Yet you, LORD, are our Father. We are the clay, you are the potter; we are all the work of your hand.
-Isaiah 64:8

Once we start to see faith as having these substantial characteristics, it gives it a more tangible reality and we can work with it a lot more easily than if we see it as an abstract idea.

Many people would say that it is faith that allows their prayers to be answered. Having faith does not give reality to unseen things; the unseen already exists. It is loyalty to unseen reality that allows it to manifest. It is believing continuously that you are what you wish to become until the imaginal state becomes stable.

Ask yourself: "Can I see the facts the world sees and still believe in the unseen state?" If you can remain loyal to the invisible state, it will eventually appear.

Faith is to believe what you do not see; the reward of this faith is to see what you believe.
-Saint Augustine

Now, if faith is the evidence of things not seen and all things are made out of things that do not appear, then we can conclude that every natural effect has a spiritual cause, and not a natural cause. There only <u>seems</u> to be a natural cause; it is a delusion of our fading, human memory. We do not remember our imaginal acts and cannot see how our experiences could have been caused by the imagination.

'All things exist, eternity exists and all things in eternity independent of creation. On this level - the shadow level - we do not see the source, the cause of it all. That is where we are called upon to exercise faith - loyalty to unseen reality. So what we now see in our world, is made out of what does not appear and we can create what we want in our world through the substance of faith.

We are called to abandon ourselves to what we love. It is an act of self-commission and we cannot commit to what we do not love… for the whole basic matter is that God is love and he exists in every one of us. We just yield completely to this presence within for by him are all things made. Through this faith, faith in the creative power of the imagination, our dreams manifest.'

Excerpt from: Faith is Loyalty to Unseen Reality (Lecture)- Neville Goddard

For whoever has it, it shall be given to him; and whoever does not have it, from him shall be taken even that which he has.
-Mark 4:25

Could 'it' be faith?

And without faith it is impossible to please God, because anyone who comes to him must believe that he exists and that he rewards those who earnestly seek him.
-Hebrews 11:6

We seek him when we turn within and rest in his presence, in his love.
By faith, we understand that the world was created by the Word of God because God calls things which are not as though they were (Romans 4:17).

An assumption though false, if persisted in, will harden into fact.

Once you know exactly what you want in this world, imagine a scene that would imply that you had it and after acting out the scene in your imagination, yield completely to the being within you to execute it; then fall asleep, convinced that he heard you.

Therefore, I tell you, whatever you ask in prayer, believe that you have received it, and it will be yours.

-Mark 11:24

Now remain loyal to that unseen reality, and observe how a bridge of incidents takes place that leads you to your desire. You are not called upon to consciously devise how this will manifest. Leave 'the how' to God. Faith is based on the power of God to externalize what you have done in your imagination.
The whole thing is finished and all you need to do is adjust to it and 'feel' yourself there until it becomes natural.

All things exist in the human imagination.
-William Blake

The imagination must be used consciously and deliberately in order to dwell in the desired state. It does not matter at the moment that external facts deny the truth of your assumption; if you persist in your assumption, it <u>will</u> become a fact.

It is not what you want that you attract, you attract what you believe to be true.
-Neville Goddard- Prayer, The Art of Believing

CREATION AND UNSEEN REALITY

All of these things are on the outside. Faith in any power other than He who is within you is false, and anyone who teaches a power on the outside is a false teacher. Christ in you is your hope of glory, and there is no other power.

The world was constructed in the mind's eye, out of things unseen by the mortal eye, and made alive by faith. Eternity exists and all things in eternity, independent of the creative act, which is the assumption of unseen reality and loyalty to its assemblage.

In spite of denial by your senses and reason, if you will be faithful to your unseen assumption, it will externalize itself. That is how all worlds come into being, but men do not understand this. Structuring their world based upon the evidence of their senses, they continue to perpetuate that which they do not desire.

Knowing what you want, close your eyes and enter its fulfillment, knowing that God is seeing what you are seeing. That He is hearing what you are saying; and what God sees and hears and remains loyal to, He externalizes.
Creation-Faith 20.05.68- Neville Goddard

Whether you imagine something or not, it already exists in the unseen. All you have to do is imagine it and remain loyal to it by resting in the new state of being. However, many base their opportunities purely on what they see around them and they are not always elevated by what they see around them.
Trust in your imagination above all things; this is where your true power lies.

2- OCCUPYING THE STATE

The whole world consists of infinite states. You are not a state, you are an immortal being who passes through different states. You enter a state and the state becomes alive.

Therefore, you are not to blame if you enter a state unwittingly and it is a horrible state.
You have to express the contents of that state. If you enter the state of poverty, you have to experience poverty. If you remain in it, you must go and drink that to the very last drop- the dregs of that cup. If you go into any state and remain in that state, you're going to drink it to the very last drop.. but you can get out of a state.
You don't have to remain in it if it's a state.

If you don't know it's a state, you identify yourself with the state and think that you're it. Man has identified himself with this little body and he thinks he is it.

Eventually the day comes, he has to discard it because he has worn it out and he discards it and all of his friends are crying to think he died. He can't die. He is an immortal being who wore a garment of flesh and blood- that same being who goes into states, remaining in a state and the state has to be expressed by him who resurrected the state for I am the Resurrection and the life of that state.

Now you can change an individual, with or without his consent if you so desire. Move yourself out of one state to another state. It all starts with a hunger- a real desire on your part and all these infinite states are simply to satisfy the hungers of men. Go into the state before you are qualified- go into the state and stay there. The state has all the things necessary to externalize itself, but you are the occupant power. You have to go into the state and dwell there.

Now, as I go into it, let me remain in it. If I come back like the positron, I'm simply going to be turned right around and deflected and continue my journey in the same direction, only deflected. I go into a state and it seems so real but when I open my eyes, I am back here and I feel shocked. That shock turns me around from that return to my motion forward now as an electron- I'm not a positron anymore. I was a positron when I actually started back in time and this body is jolted when I open my eyes. What I did there is I moved across a bridge of incidents, some series of events that leads me up to the fulfilment of my desires in what the world calls reality.

But it was real when I occupied it in my imagination. That's when it was real.

We exist in these bodies… we live in our imaginations. For our imaginations, these are the only realities.
Imagination is God, the Divine Body, Jesus.
Justified states, 1969- Neville Goddard

In this talk, Neville Goddard spoke of how we are all immortal beings who pass through different states and in doing so, change our individual worlds and experiences. Everyone is forgiven everything they have ever done or will ever do as it is God who has created these states. People do not know this and so condemn the person when they have done something considered wrong when in fact, they are merely acting out the state they have entered.

The occupant of the rich state does not differ from the occupant of the poor state. One is not better than the other in the eyes of God. All are acquitted as they are only expressing a state and are unable to do otherwise.

Divine acquittal is justification. Glorification follows, which is the gift of God himself to you. God gives you the Kingdom which is not a realm but a character. You do not earn it- it is an unmerited gift and the gift is nothing less than God himself. Your fitness for the kingdom is the consequence not the condition of this gift.

Man matures when he becomes his own father which is the unfolding of God within you and his

Son, Jesus Christ. This is the hope that unfolds into wisdom to endure the burden of this long, dark night of time.

The apostle, Paul said, 'For I consider that the sufferings of this present time are not worthy to be compared with the glory which shall be revealed in us.' (Romans 8:18)

There is nothing but God in this world. You inherit God and God owns the world and the world is your inheritance. We inherit the earth. The whole drama of life moves from the heavenly state of innocence to a world of experience of educative darkness to awakened imagination.

William Blake said, "I realize that neither the just nor the wicked are in a Supreme state, but to be every one of them States of the sleep, which the soul may fall into; its deadly dreams of good and evil."

So how do you occupy a state? By changing your concept of self. By asking yourself how you would feel, what you would see, hear, touch, taste, and smell and how you would move. Contemplate the state because the moment you contemplate it, you become the very thing you are imagining. Write your own script and act it out in your imagination.

SCIENTIFIC PARALLELS- THE POSITRON

Professor Feynman, of Cornell University, one of the outstanding physicists of the day in speculative, theoretical physics, wrote a letter for the publication- The Science Newsletter (October 15th 1949)- concerning the positron, a particle produced in atomic disintegration which is like the electron but positive in its charge. Almost 20 years later he received the Nobel Prize for his 1949 paper, 'The Theory of Positrons'.

Feynman stated:
"The positron is a wrong-way electron. It starts from where it hasn't been, and it speeds to where it was an instant ago. It is bounced so hard its time sense is reversed, and then it returns to where it hasn't been.
When a little electron is moving speedily in space if it is bounced, it's deflected, but continues on its course. But if it is bounced so hard, then its time sense is reversed, and it returns to where it hasn't been."

"Now," he said, "on the basis of this, we must now conclude that the entire concept that man held of the universe is false. We always believed that the future developed slowly out of the past. Now, with this concept which we have seen and photographed, we must now conclude that the entire space-time history of the world is laid out, and we only become aware of increasing portions of it successively."

Both views are comparable:
Dr. Richard Feynman: "The positron starts from where it hasn't been, and it moves to where it was a moment before; arriving there, it is bounced so hard, its time sense is reversed, and it moves back to where it hasn't been."

Neville Goddard: "I go forward in time to where I have not yet visited physically, and I simply enclose myself in the feeling of the wish fulfilled. I haven't yet realized it physically, but I go forward in my mind's eye, in my imagination, into the state, and I talk with my friends from the wish fulfilled as though it were true. Then I open my eyes and I am startled to find that I am sitting in a chair where I was a moment before. And what I have just done is denied by my senses, but strangely enough, the whole vast world reshuffles itself and forms a bridge of incidents, across which I move to the fulfilment of that state where I have been."

"I went forward and I did what I wanted to do. And then I started from where I had not been physically, and sped back to where I was physically; and then I was bounced – shocked – that it wasn't true. I was bounced so hard that I then turned around in my time sense and moved back to fulfil where I had been in my imagination.

If there is evidence for a thing, does it really matter what the world thinks about it, if there is evidence for it? Well, I had the evidence for it, but I could not explain it scientifically. I only knew that it worked."
Neville Goddard

CONSCIOUSNESS- THE LORD FROM HEAVEN

We have only to enlarge our conception of causality, to excuse everything and forgive all.

In your limbs lie nations twain, rival races from their birth. One the mastery will gain, the younger o'er the elder reign.
Genesis 25

The first one is the sense man, my normal apprehension of corporeal objects, that which is not present and yet I perceive them, I call that imagination. That is destined to rule. That is the second man, the Lord from heaven. The first man is of the earth, a man of dust, the second is from heaven. So here we are in this world and this is the world of this dual state within every child born of woman. And so we have the physical man, the man of dust and then we have the spiritual man, the man of imagination that is the immortal man. When I see this picture of the duality of man and how all things are created by this hidden man, I forgive everything in this world that the physical man does, for the physical man is only a state. One being is playing all the parts. The part played by the thief is the same being playing the part of the judge who judges the thief. The part who is the murderer and the murdered is a part but the being within is one.

There are infinite states in this world and all you have to do is forget states. You play your part and every state necessary to make your part come to fulfilment will be present at the moment you need it.

To understand this world, you must think in terms of states.

'He has made everything for its purpose, even the wicked for the time of trouble.'

When the inner man begins to awake, he selects his part wisely.
Everything in this world that you want to be, you can be if you know that there are only states. You move into the state because the occupant of the state does not differ from the occupant of any other state.

So, all we have to do is expand a little bit, our conception of causality to excuse everything and forgive everyone in this world.
Forgive them as they are instrumental in fulfilling your dream.

Now, what do I want in place of what my senses are telling me. Let me now enter into that state and live it as though it were true and move forward in that state.

An idea that is only an idea produces nothing and does nothing. It must be felt so that it awakens within oneself certain sensations, certain motor actions in order to be effective. What would the feeling be like if it were true? Dwell upon that until the feeling awakes within you these sensations for imagination is spiritual sensation. That is the creative being in you. It's not just to entertain an idea. What idea? the idea must produce within you this feeling which is a sensation. What would the feeling be like if it were true? You dwell upon that until you catch that feeling. As Churchill said the mood determines the fortunes of people rather than the fortunes the mood. The mood precedes the fortunes.

So, what would you want in this world? Well, contemplate it. What would the feeling be like if you had it? What would it be like if it were true? That is the story of scripture. If I could only feel that I am already the man that I want to be, that I am already the woman that I want to be and feel it then it is not only an idea, which as an idea without feeling will produce nothing.
<u>*The secret is in the feeling.*</u>
The Duality of Man, edited- Neville Goddard

CONSCIOUSNESS

'The sperm somehow easily passes through the surface of an egg although the outside of the egg has no holes in it either before or after fertilization.

…There are these unnumbered states of consciousness- you can liken each state to an egg and every state remains just like the egg until fertilized and the presence that fertilizes the egg is simply our consciousness.

We must be in it to activate it, to animate it. You could this very moment single out any state and by the use of your imagination, imagine that you're in it.

You really are where you are imagining yourself to be. For man, being all imagination, he must be where he is in imagination. You will find yourself compelled to move across a bridge of incident leading up to the fulfilment of that state.'
Edited from-The Secret of the Sperm, 1965- Neville Goddard

Consciousness is not divisional. There is no separation in consciousness. 'I AM' cannot be divided. Whatever you conceive yourself to be, the center of your being remains the same regardless of the concept you hold of yourself.

Two thoughts emerge for me on this subject: Is there only me in this world and everyone I experience is the result of my concept of myself?
AND
Are we all manifestations of God, imagining different circumstances for ourselves and therefore having an effect on everyone else's imagination?

One thought suggests everything that happens to me comes from me. The other thought suggests we are partially responsible for our worlds, but the imaginations of others have an effect. One thought says there is no one to blame, the other that people have an effect on our life. Most people behave according to the latter idea no matter what they believe. It takes a concerted effort to cultivate an attitude of no-blame towards others no matter how the circumstances appear. In a sense, both ideas are true. We are all one in God and we are all having an impact upon each other but essentially everything that manifests in this world comes from the same source, therefore there is no one to blame.

This is where Neville Goddard tells us that we have only to 'enlarge our conception of causality to forgive everyone in our world.' In other words, understand that everything is coming from one source, God.

If we are consciously placing ourselves into the state of the wish fulfilled and imagining ourselves to be the person we wish to be, we can have confidence that everything that appears in our world will lead us to the desired goal. We cross a bridge of incidents that lead to the desired state. If some of those incidents are not pleasant, pay no heed, for 'his ways are far above our ways.' (Isaiah 55) The 'how' is not for us to know, we are to have faith that 'it is done' and that is all. If we can believe that all things already exist and we have only to believe them into existence, then it is as good as done in the future, which is only a construct of the mind. We can bring the future to the present moment by remaining loyal to faith in the world of the invisible.

We can have full control over our destiny. The key factor in having success is faith.

To feel aware is to feel 'I AM'.
I AM is the cause-substance which manifests different arrangements into the world depending on how we perceive ourselves to be. If 'I AM', 'awareness' conceives itself to be rich, eventually its environment will reflect that assumption. If 'I AM' conceives itself to be deeply loved, eventually this belief will be manifested through the arrangement of the cause-substance and loving relationships will be reflected back to the individual who assumes he or she is loved.

Consciousness is the life-force that ignites the state into being. There are infinite states in the world and all we have to do is choose which state we wish to live in and dwell in it as if it were so because it IS so and the reality of the sense world will begin to form from our particular arrangement of the cause substance. Change your concept of yourself and you change your world.

Consciousness is the only reality and therefore the only substance.
There is only consciousness operating in the world; the world has no motive of its own. What you believe to be true is what you shall experience in this world.
Ask yourself:

What is your concept of yourself?

Define the person you want to be and become it. Live in this new concept and it will manifest through the new arrangement of your mind in your world. Rearrange your mind and live in the new self-concept. If you become it, you will see your world change to reflect your new concept of self.

This cannot fail because you and your world are one.

3. PERSIST IN THE ASSUMPTION

Define your ideal and concentrate your attention upon the idea of identifying yourself with your ideal. Assume the feeling of being it, the feeling that would be yours were you already the embodiment of your ideal. Then live and act upon this conviction. This assumption, though denied by the senses, if persisted in, will become fact. You will know when you have succeeded in fixing the desired state in consciousness by simply looking mentally at the people you know. In dialogues with yourself you are less inhibited and more sincere than in actual conversations with others, therefore the opportunity for self-analysis arises when you are surprised by your mental conversations with others. If you see them as you formerly saw them, you have not changed your concept of self, for all changes of concepts of self, result in a changed relationship to your world.
(Ch2- Out of this World- Neville Goddard)

This is a vital point that Neville Goddard makes in his book, 'Out of this World.' If you have truly changed your concept of yourself, you have changed your relationship to others and you will notice when communication is not as you would expect it to be in the world. Self-analysis is seen as an opportunity and there is an indication that this may take us closer to the new concept we wish to embody.

We must always include people in our imaginal acts and see them relating to us in the new state. This will gradually become the case in objective reality. You must assume you are already the person you wish to be as you can only know a thing spiritually by becoming it.

And be not conformed to this world: but be ye transformed by the renewing of your mind, that ye may prove what is the good, and acceptable, and perfect, will of God.
Romans 12:2

Your mind can only be renewed by changing your thoughts which means thinking from NEW IDEAS. As your new concept of self takes root, you will naturally think of ideas that come from the new state. Allow these ideas to grow and contemplate them as definite possibilities and opportunities to consider.

It is always through the imagination that you bring your present world into being. The material evidence of the imagination follows it, as its shadow.

This new state of consciousness will manifest as you persist in the assumption.

Do not long to become a certain state but dwell in it through the use of the imagination. Do not feel a hunger-like desire for your dream to be fulfilled but instead feel satisfied that it IS already so.
It is like playing make-believe as a child. You play with the idea that you are already that person and THINK from the new state. It involves deliberate, conscious control of the imagination. You identify yourself with the idea and become transformed into its image.

Claim that you are what you want to be. Persist in that assumption. If this assumption is persisted in until it becomes your dominant feeling, the attainment of your ideal is inevitable.

In order to develop the habit of assuming, commit yourself to these words before sleep for one week:

I assume I am _____ (the one I want to be). I claim it from the invisible and know it is coming into my world very soon.

Fall asleep assuming it is true.

Believe in yourself.

Persist in the assumption that you are already the person you would like to be and then live by faith that you are already in that state.

RELAX

When you assume, keep a relaxed attention on the feeling of the wish fulfilled.

Everything already exists in the invisible. We cannot see it as we can only view contents of our own consciousness as we dwell in our current state.
'It is the function of an assumption to call back the excluded view and restore full vision.' (*The Power of Awareness- Neville Goddard)*

You see with the eye of God, the imagination, and bring the invisible into sight. Your assumption then guides your movements and causes a bridge of incidents to take place that leads to your end goal.
When you rest in the assumption that you already are what you want to be, you and your Infinite Being are merged in creative unity and God never fails. Master your assumptions and master life.

Surrender to the assumption by identifying with the new conception of self. Yield to the feeling of the wish fulfilled and be consumed as its victim then rise in the new state.

Confidence in your assumptions is the single most important thing you can do to ensure your dreams become reality.

Disregard all evidence that denies the fulfillment of your desire and remain sure it is on the way. We live in an assumptive world. Everything that exists has come about through our expectations and assumptions, consciously but more often unconsciously.

'You win by assumption what you can never win by force. An assumption is a certain motion of consciousness. This motion exercises an influence on the surrounding substance causing it to take the shape of and reflect back the assumption. A change in the arrangement of consciousness brings about a new direction.'
(The Power of Awareness- Neville Goddard)

What we send out, comes back to us. Our future is molded through our concept of self.

It must, however, be stated that although we have infinite free will in choosing our assumptions, we have no power to determine conditions and events. This is why we should keep an open mind when <u>seemingly</u> negative events enter into our lives as we do not know the route we are taking to our destination.

Whatsoever things are pure, just, lovely, of good report- think on these things.

Why does it feel so bad to occupy our minds with negativity?
It feels bad in the center of your gut- a nervous, jittery feeling that won't let you be and reminds you regularly that it is still there. It wants you to deal with it so that it can be released and you can feel what you truly are - love. Negativity is like poison to the core of our being and blocks what we truly are. We need to deal with it and we do this by contemplating the above scripture and acting through love.

No matter what people are like, try and see the best in them and know that this is the truth. Focus on this and feel good by developing deeper, more meaningful relationships where people feel good to be around you as they feel accepted and liked in your eyes. Alternatively, you could focus on their flaws and get lost in endless judgement as you retract from all social contact with the person in question. If we remain open to a feeling of love, we will enjoy better contact with others and bring better situations our way. So- 'Whatsoever things are pure, just, lovely, of good report- think on these things.' Remember this scripture when your mind turns to the negative.

Assume the best and persist in your assumptions. Remind yourself every day that you are what you want to be, that you have what you want to have and take it as fact. This idea

exists in the imagination which means it can be brought to life by mere assumption. Faith is loyalty to invisible reality.
Persist in believing in your imagined reality and it WILL manifest as objective reality.

Never forget that **assumptions harden into facts.**

CONCLUSION-PERSEVERANCE

Persevere in your assumption of the wish fulfilled and it will come to pass. Perseverance means maintaining the consciousness of being who we want to be. We remain in the state of the wish fulfilled as often as we can until we feel that we are that which we wish to be.
It is a maintained attitude of being.

If you remain in me and my words remain in you, ask whatever you wish and it will be done for you. **John 15:7**

Meditate on the words of scripture. Find passages that speak of faith and prayer and contemplate the wisdom that lies within them. The meaning will penetrate deeper into your soul and you will gain understanding enabling you to persevere. This scripture will then be fulfilled in you and may ask whatever you wish and it will be done for you.

Count it all joy, my brothers, when you meet with trials of various kinds, for you know that the testing of your faith produces steadfastness. And let steadfastness have its full effect, that you

may be perfect and complete, lacking in nothing.
James 1:2-4

Do not be swayed by misfortune but rest in the desired state and believe that you have already received. If you remain steadfast in your faith, steadfast in your new concept of yourself, you will receive what you have imagined and want for nothing.

For you have need of endurance, so that when you have done the will of God, you may receive what is promised.
Hebrews 10:36

God puts his desires in your heart for you to fulfil them. God also asks us to love one another as we love ourselves. Through love, we receive what is promised.

But the one who looks into the perfect law, the law of liberty, and perseveres being no hearer who forgets but a doer who acts, he will be blessed in his doing.
James 1:25

The law of liberty is to believe that you receive and you shall have it. We are all hearers who forget due to our fading, 'vegetable memories'. We must act and we act by creating an imaginal act which signifies that we have achieved our aim and we put ourselves in the scene, seeing, hearing moving, touching, using all our senses to feel as though we are there now. We carry the feeling around with us and think from the new concept of self.

Do not be conformed to this world, but be transformed by the renewal of your mind, that by testing you may discern what is the will of God, what is good and acceptable and perfect.
Romans 12:2

Do not let the world control you but control your world by using your imagination to manifest consciously. It is the will of God for you to be a creator as he is the creator and as you mold the world through the power within you, you will discover what the will of God is for your life. God is the all-good and there is nothing within him that is not perfect. It is for you to become like him…

Do not give up but retain a relaxed assumption that you are already the person you desire to be.

The vision has its own appointed hour, it ripens, it will flower. If it be long, then wait, it is sure and will not be late. **Habbukuk 2:3**

Every conception of a desire has its own appointed hour and will not be late- relative to its own nature. We see this reflected in the world where there are different periods of gestation between conception and birth. A child takes nine months, a lamb five, a chicken twenty-one days and an elephant over a year. The length of time it takes the desired state to appear in the world is a mystery but the more natural the feeling of the state desired, the quicker it will manifest.

It is imperative that you remain patient and continue to dwell in the feeling of the wish fulfilled which means building positive habits of study and imagining until it becomes second nature to you; it also means continuing with this indefinitely. In time, it will become less of an effort and more of a way of life. It is a happier and more fulfilling way of being and will produce the fruit of your imagining. Patience, persistence and faith are key in this new adventure you are embarking on.

Remember: you are the operant power; it doesn't operate itself!

Trust in your imagination above all things; this is where your true power lies.

Wishing you great success...

QUOTES TO INSPIRE

Imagination and faith are the secrets of creation.
Neville Goddard (Resurrection)

The eternal body of man is the imagination, and that is God Himself.
William Blake

The mood determines the fortunes of people rather than the fortunes determine the mood.
Winston Churchill

Imagination is everything. It is the preview of life's coming attractions.
Albert Einstein

Everything you can imagine is real.
Pablo Picasso

The world is but a canvas to the imagination
Henry David Thoreau

The man who has no imagination, has no wings
Muhammad Ali

Anyone who lives within their means suffers from a lack of imagination.
Oscar Wilde

Reality leaves a lot to the imagination.
John Lennon

Imagination is the only weapon in the war against reality.
Lewis Carroll- Alice in Wonderland

…the imagination of nature is far, far greater than the imagination of man.
Richard Feynman

They who dream by day are cognizant of many things which escape those who dream only by night.
Edgar Allan Poe (Eleonora)

Imagination governs the world.
Napoleon Bonaparte

Imagination has given us the steam engine, the telephone, the talking-machine, and the automobile, for these things had to be dreamed of before they became realities.
L. Frank Baum (The Lost Princess of Oz)

All that you behold, though it appears without, it is within, in your imagination of which this world of mortality is but a shadow.
William Blake

EXPERIENCES

There are only two ways we create in our world; consciously and unconsciously.

Examples of creating consciously from the lectures of Neville Goddard

1- Barbados

(Neville Goddard - edited from 'Out of this World: Thinking Fourth-Dimensionally (1948) - Lesson 3)

Let me tell you why I am doing what I am doing today. It was back in 1933 in the city of New York, and my old friend Abdullah, with whom I studied Hebrew for five years, was really the beginning of the eating of all my superstitions. When I went to him, I was filled with superstitions. I could not eat meat, I could not eat fish, I could not eat chicken, I could not eat any of these things that were living in the world. I did not drink, I did not smoke, and I was making a tremendous effort to live a celibate life.

Abdullah said to me, "I am not going to tell you, 'You are crazy, Neville', but you are you know. All these things are stupid." But I could not believe they were stupid.

In November, 1933, I bade goodbye to my parents in the city of New York as they sailed for Barbados. I had been in this country 12 years with no desire to see Barbados. I was not successful and I was ashamed to go home to successful members of my family. After 12 years in America, I was a failure in my own eyes. I was in the theatre and made money one year and spent it the next month. I was not what I would call by their standards nor by mine, a successful person.

Mind you, when I said goodbye to my parents in November, I had no desire to go to Barbados. The ship pulled out, and as I came up the street, something possessed me with a desire to go to Barbados.

It was the year 1933, I was unemployed and had no place to go except a little room on 75th Street. I went straight to my old friend Abdullah and said to him, "Ab, the strangest feeling is possessing me. For the first time in 12 years, I want to go to Barbados."
"If you want to go Neville, you have gone." he replied. That was very strange language to me. I am in New York City on 72nd Street and he tells me I have gone to Barbados. I said to him, "What do you mean, I have gone, Abdullah?"
He said, "Do you really want to go?"
I answered, "Yes."

He then said to me, "As you walk through this door now, you are not walking on 72nd Street, you are walking on palm-lined streets, coconut-lined streets- this is Barbados. Do not ask me how you are going to go. You are in Barbados. You do not say 'how' when you are there. You are there. Now you walk as though you were there."
I went out of his place in a daze. I am in Barbados. I have no money, I have no job, I am not even well clothed, and yet I am in Barbados.

He was not the kind of a person with whom you would argue- not Abdullah. Two weeks later I was no nearer my goal than on the day I first told him I wanted to go to Barbados. I said to him, "Ab, I trust you implicitly but here is one time I cannot see how it is going to work. I have not one penny towards my journey." I began to explain…

You know what he did? As I sat in his living room, he rose from his chair and went towards his study and slammed the door, which was not an invitation to follow him. As he went through the door he said to me, "I have said all that I have to say."

On the 3rd of December I stood before Abdullah and told him again I was no nearer my trip. He repeated his statement, "You are in Barbados."

The very last ship sailing for Barbados that would take me there for the reason I wanted to go, which was to be there for Christmas, sailed at noon on December 6th, 'the old Nerissa'. On the morning of December 4th, having no job, having no place to go, I slept late. When I got up there was an air mail letter from Barbados under my door. As I opened the letter a little piece of paper flickered to the floor. I picked it up and it was a draft for $50

The letter was from my brother Victor and it read, "I am not asking you to come, Neville, this is a command. We have never had a Christmas when all the members of our family were present at the same time. This Christmas it could be done if you would come."

My oldest brother Cecil left home before the youngest was born and then we started to move away from home at different times so never in the history of our family were we ever all together at the same time.

The letter continued… "You are not working; I know there is no reason why you cannot come, so you must be here before Christmas. The enclosed $50 is to buy a few shirts or a pair of shoes you may need for the trip. You will not need tips; use the bar if you are drinking. I will meet the ship and pay all your tips and your incurred expenses. I have cabled Furness, Withy & Co. in New York City and told them to issue you a ticket when you appear at their office. The $50 is simply to buy some little essentials. You may sign as you want aboard the ship. I will meet it and take care of all obligations."

I went down to Furness, Withy & Co. with my letter and let them read it. They said, "We received the cable, Mr. Goddard but unfortunately we have not any space left on the December 6th sailing. The only thing available is Third Class between New York and St. Thomas. When we get to St. Thomas, we have a few passengers who are getting off- you may then ride First Class from St. Thomas to Barbados. But between New York and St. Thomas you must go

Third Class, although you may have the privileges of the First-Class dining room and walk the decks of the First Class."
I said, "I will take it."

I went back to my friend Abdullah on the afternoon of December 4th and said, "It worked like a dream!" I told him what I had done, thinking he would be happy.
Do you know what he said to me? He said, "Who told you that you are going Third Class? Did I see you in Barbados, the man you are, going Third Class? You are in Barbados and you went there First Class!"

I did not have one moment to see him again before I sailed at noon on December 6th. When I reached the dock with my passport and my papers to get aboard that ship the agent said to me, "We have good news for you, Mr. Goddard. There has been a cancellation and you are going First Class."
Abdullah taught me the importance of remaining faithful to an idea and not compromising. I wavered, but he remained faithful to the assumption that I was in Barbados and had traveled First Class.

2- Drafted into the Army

(Neville Goddard - edited from 'The Perfect Law of Liberty' -2 April 1971)

If you are sent to jail for ten years, then maybe you get off in six for good behavior, but when you are drafted into the Army, there is no date that you are promised where they let you out. You are in for the duration.

Well, I was drafted into the Army among seventeen million of us. Well, I didn't ask the permission of anyone, I only consulted myself. I looked around, and I knew what the world knows; it was something that had to be done. But I must be honest with myself; I didn't want any part of it! Others would tell me, "Is that the act of a coward?" I didn't care what they said – "Is that being a good citizen?" I didn't care what they said.

We are at war, and we are all Americans. We should be going there because our country has declared war and so 'reason' tells us that should be done.

When I was drafted, I did not oppose it. They drafted me. They took me down to Camp Polk, Louisiana, for my basic training, and while I was there, I didn't want any part of it, and I dared to assume that I'm out of it. I made my normal, natural application, as you have to do in the world and within 24 hours it came back and it was simply rejected. It was signed, "Disapproved," and signed by my Colonel, a very nice gentleman. His name was Colonel Theodore Bilboe, Jr. His father was Senator from Mississippi. I said nothing.

My Captain said, "For your sake, Goddard, I am very, very sorry. I know exactly how you feel. You want to be with your wife and little girl. Your son is in Guadalcanal with the Marines, and you are now almost 38 years old, and so I know, but I would like to go through this war with a man just like you at my side. So, I can't say that I am sorry for myself- I am sorry only for you."

I didn't say one word to him, or to the Colonel; I didn't oppose it. I looked into the perfect law, 'the law of liberty,' and I persevered in that law and I slept that night as though I slept in my own home in New York City on Washington Square, where I lived on the 7th floor. I lived on that floor. It was a very large apartment – two bedrooms, a lovely big living room, a dining room, a huge kitchen, and the foyer- and I slept in that place just as though I were there and not in the Army. I fell asleep in that state, having done all the normal things that would make me feel this arrangement is perfect. I rearranged the structure of my mind. Instead of seeing 25 men around me sleeping upstairs and knowing that there were 25 down below in the next area, I slept in my own bed with my wife in her bed and my little girl in her crib in the corner. I felt everything in that place just as though it's taking place, and I rearranged the structure of my mind, and fell sound asleep in that state.

At 4 o'clock in the morning, a sheet of paper appeared before my eyes and a hand came down with a pen in its hand, and the pen scratched out the word 'disapproved' and it wrote in, in a bold script, 'approved'. And then I heard the words: "That which I have done, I have done. Do nothing!" and then I awoke. It was too early to disturb the 25 other fellows sleeping there, and I waited until the very first moment that I could leave that room, and went down to the latrine and shaved and bathed early, and came up filled with a glow that the whole thing was done. I walked in that assumption for the next nine days.

Nine days later, the same Colonel that disapproved my request called me in. He said, "Close the door, Goddard," so I closed the door. He said, "Take a seat." He'd never asked me to take a seat in his presence before. I was a private. You always stood in his presence, and never took a seat. Then he gave me all the reasons in the world why I should still be in the Army.

He said, "Do you still want to get out?"

I said, "Yes, Sir."

He gave me another reason. "Do you still want to get out?"

I said, "Yes, Sir."

Another one; and when he exhausted all the reasons why I should be in the Army, I was still saying, "Yes, Sir."

He said, "All right, bring me another application and have your Captain sign it," which I did. And that day I was honorably discharged and out of the Army. I didn't run away; I was honorably discharged.

When vision breaks forth into speech, the presence of Deity is assured and who can oppose God? He said, "That which I have done, I have done. Do nothing!"

So, he thought he initiated the urge to let me go free. I looked into the perfect law, the law of liberty, and I persevered in that law; and he played his part, for I rearranged the structure of my mind.

I was convinced I wanted out, and I didn't ask any one's permission. I did not discuss it with anyone as to why I should want out when seventeen million are being drafted, plus numberless girls to make a tremendous effort against this monstrous thing that was going on in Europe. I still wanted out. I did not take any one into my confidence as to why I wanted out. I had my 13-weeks basic training, and then when I came out, they gave me my citizenship papers. Back in 1922, I could have been an American, but I just didn't have the time or the urge to get around to become a citizen so I drifted on and drifted on and drifted on until after this little episode. That's why I went into the Army, or I would still be drifting through, being a citizen of Britain. But now I'm an American by adoption and they gave it to me because I did fulfil a 13-week training course in the American Army.

So, I tell you, I know from experience how true this statement in James is. Read it carefully: 'Be doers of the word, and not hearers only, deceiving yourself. For he who is a hearer of the word, and not a doer, he is like one who looks into the mirror and sees his natural face; and then he goes away and at once forgets what he looks like. But he who is a doer, he looks into the perfect law, the law of liberty, and perseveres. And when he does that, he is blessed in his doing.'

That is, acting – making the thing become alive within you. Now, he tells us in the same chapter- 'Faith without works is dead, as the body, apart from the spirit is dead'- so faith without works is dead.
He is not proposing that I substitute works for faith. Works are the evidence whether the faith I profess is alive or dead. I say I believe the story of Scripture. Well then, if I believe it, then do it! He said, 'Whatever you desire, believe you have received, and you shall.' If I really believe that – I can't say I believe by quoting the Apostle's Creed. That's not belief. Going to church and genuflecting before some man-made little cross – that's not scripture. Do you really believe the doctrines, the teachings, of scripture? Not the traditions of men, not the rituals, not the outer ceremonies; but the teachings of scripture – 'When you pray, believe that you have received, and you will.' And, 'All things are possible to him who believes.' Well, do I believe that? Well then, believe it!

If I really believe that I am out of the Army, what and where would I be? Well, I would be at home, in my place a thousand miles away, on Washington Square. If I looked through the window, I would see the Holly Apartments, if I looked to the left, I would see Washington Square, if I looked to the right, I would see Sixth Avenue – it's now called the Avenue of the Americas, but it's still Sixth Avenue to me. And there, I would look at Sixth Avenue. Well, I did that, that night. I saw Sixth Avenue, I saw Washington Square, and then I went through the entire apartment and touched objects with my imaginary hands.

Now, was that rational? The world would say that was the most irrational thing that one can do. Now, what is reason? The office of reason is simply to extract conclusions from premises. Must my premises always be based upon the evidence of my senses? Must they always dictate what is rational to me? Well, having done this, and proved it to be a fact, reason doesn't mean to me what it means to the world.

3- Using the imagination to acquire a building

(Neville Goddard - edited from 'Live in the End' -19 July 1968)

Who knows what you are imagining? No one knows, but you can sit down and imagine, and no one can stop you from doing it, but can you give reality to the imagined state? If you do, yes, a bridge of incidents will appear in your world, and you'll walk across some series of events leading up to the fulfilment of

the imaginal state. But don't give causation to any physical step that you took towards the fulfilment of it. You imagine yourself having a marvelous business, and then comes the day a building is for sale and you haven't a nickel towards it, and a total, not a total stranger, but a man comes in and asks you quite in a friendly manner, "Are you going to buy it?" And knowing you don't have a penny, you say to him, as you would a friend to a friend, "With what?" And then he says, "Well, I have money. It's only in the bank drawing nothing." You say, "Well, I have no collateral." But he says, "I've watched you. You are an honest person, your family- they are honest- I think they are. Would you like me to buy it for you and get my lawyer to bid for it? If they knew that I am bidding, they know that I have money, they will bid me up, and so I'll get it at the very lowest price by getting a lawyer who represents more than one client, and they do not know who he represents, and he'll bid for it. Are you willing to take it, regardless of the price?" and you say, "Yes, I'll take it, but I have no collateral."
"All I need is your signature that you will simply pay six percent on whatever the price is, and then reduce that principal over a period of ten years. Agreed?"
"Yes."
"Well, then, sign this, and we'll see if we can buy it." That day you own the building, and you didn't have one nickel when you owned the building that day! You only had your signature on a piece of paper. At the end of 10 years, you repay the man his principal; you reduce it every year, paying him six percent on the remaining principal, and reduce the entire thing at the end of ten years.

That man dies twenty years later and leaves you $150,000 in cash, tax free, and a couple of homes and many personal belongings. In the meanwhile, you continue in that business, and it multiplies and multiplies, and that year was 1924. This is now 1968. That building - I'm speaking factually - that building in 1924 is now gone. He paid only $50,000 for it. It was repaid and repaid. A bank - three years ago, bought the property. The building was rotted - bought the property for $840,000 in cash, and no capital gain. From $50,000 to $840,000! In the meanwhile, the business has expanded into all the other islands, so that today you couldn't buy them out for 15 million dollars! All in imagination! And this goes back to the imagination that preceded this man's offer to buy the building for the young man, seeing this building and entertaining the thought that the present owners deceived his father, and through deception got him out of a partnership - a junior partnership. And he was moved, not to get even, but to prove that he really had something within him and could be a success, in spite of their deception.

So, every day he would see on that marquee, not their name, but his own family's name, and he would see it in his mind's eye, because you could not take their name and transliterate it and make it spell this man's family's name, but he saw it. In his mind's eye he saw that name, which if true would imply the family owned it. He did it every day, twice a day, for two years, and then came this, suddenly, out of the nowhere, and the whole thing was made possible, and today they are all over the islands, and they have no partners. They have never taken in one partner, never sold one bit of stock outside of the family ownership. All by imagination!

Now, I know what I'm talking about because I'm a member of that family. I am speaking of my own family. This is not hearsay. I know it. My second brother, Victor, was the one in whose imagination this whole thing began to bloom and he still works all by imagination. He knows what he wants and then after having decided in himself, "That's what I want, and that's good for the business," he then, in his mind's eye, appropriates it, and then lets things happen. As told us in Scripture,

The vision has its own appointed hour,
It ripens, it will flower; if it be long, then wait,
For it is sure, and it will not be late.
Habakkuk 2:3 - Moffat's translation

Read that in the book of Habakkuk. Here is the true translation of that passage in Habakkuk.
So, when you know what you want, remain faithful to that assumption, and the assumption- though at the moment is denied by your senses, and denied by reason- if you persist in it, it will harden into fact. Are we not told that God calls a thing that is not seen as though it were seen, and then the unseen becomes seen? (Romans 4:17) He calls everything from the unseen into the seen in this simple manner, for he is the resurrecting power.
So, if I assume that 'I AM', I don't have to have evidence to support it. I assume that 'I AM' - am what? - well, I name it, and having given it a name, given it form, given it definition, remaining in it, I resurrect it. And if it takes a thousand men to aid the birth of that state, a thousand men will play their parts, and I don't have to go out and look for them, any more than my brother had to go out and look for this man. He would not have known where to start

looking for one the day of the sale. So far as he is concerned, he had done it in his mind's eye, and he allowed everything to happen, and he comes right in like a joke. He really thought it was a joke, and he said to this man, "Are you fooling me?"
He said, "No."
He said, "Well then, wait. Let me call my father- he's at lunch." He called him on the wire. He said, "Daddy, come on up. Leave everything and come." And then he said, "Now, you tell my father what you told me."
My father's name is Joseph, and my father said, "You really mean it?"
He said, "Yes, Joe, I mean it. I'll have him bid today. You put your signature here and your son Victor put his signature- that's all I need."
And that was a lifetime friendship. So, when that man died, he didn't owe my brother Victor anything. He so loved the friendship and the feeling of, well, decency that he had with my brother Victor. He gave him $150,000 in cash, and that was tax free, and the homes. Everything was tax free. And that building which he bought for $50,000 was sold three years ago to the Bank of Nova Scotia. They tore it down and built a lovely structure but they paid our family $840,000 for that building, and there was no capital tax gain. The whole thing was simply free.

So, I know what I'm talking about. All I need from you is the acceptance of it. Will you believe it? Will you believe that with God all things are possible? (Mark 10:27) Will you believe that all things are possible to man?

Well, you can prove it in the not-distant future, but you are the operant power. It will not work itself. If you dare to assume this very night that you have a better job than you now hold or that you have a larger income… you may be fired tomorrow… don't be concerned! On reflection, you'll see it was necessary to move you towards the fulfilment of your assumption. You could be fired! And I wouldn't bat an eye if you told me tomorrow, "Well, I did what you told me. You know what happened? I was fired!"

I have seen that. It takes someone to fire you to get you into a better job. I have seen that time and again. I wouldn't go out and quit the job. You may be promoted in the job, or you may be invited by some other concern that is competitive to join them- I do not know how it happens- I only know if you remain faithful to the assumption, it's going to happen and you are going to be promoted towards the fulfilment of the state that you've dared to assume that is yours.

I could tell you unnumbered stories along this nature. So, here, I say, "Dwell in the end… the end is where we begin," for if I've seen my name on the marquee, that's the end. I don't wait for the incident to take place in my world to move from one to the other to the other, leading up to that; I dwell in the end. So, if I go to the very end… what would it be like, were it true?

Again, I say unto you, that if two of you shall agree on earth as touching anything that they shall ask, it shall be done for them of my Father which is in heaven.
- Matthew 18:19

The two that have to agree are the Word and the Mind. Jesus is the Word and the Mind is the presence of I AM- God.

We speak our desire in our heads or out loud and if we have faith in what we say, there is a point when our sense of being, our I AM agrees. Our desire has been touched within us and a feeling of peace and contentment follows as that desire is satiated. We know that we have it and we carry it with us without effort. It then manifests in the world.

The more we pay attention to the seeming coincidences in our lives and make connections with our first thoughts of them, the more our faith will increase and we will practice this with less and less effort. The more relaxed and confident we become, the more easily we will manifest. We can live in abundance with a generosity that lives in gratitude to this power and trusts in God's love for us. With less clinging to desires, there can be an openness and deeper love of God and humankind. It will not lead to greed and miserliness if understood and practiced properly but instead will lead to a life filled with more love and a desire to help others.

Margaret Ruth Broome on Neville Goddard

It's been almost twenty years since I sat in the auditorium of the Women's Club in Los Angeles, California and watched a man in a gray pinstriped suit walk out on the stage and take his place behind the podium where many tape recorders were placed across the stage. A man would walk by, press the buttons of the many machines, sit down and the speaker would begin.

I have blessed my recorder many times for, although I attended the hour-long lectures for seven years, when I heard the words, "Now let us go into the silence," I could not recall one word that had been said.

Neville always had the power to take me with him. (Perhaps because I was always eager and willing to go). I seemed to have no control, but would simply be transformed by his words and allow him to take me to experience sights and sounds I never before knew existed. Yet they were all so familiar that my heart sang the Hallelujah Chorus.

The hour was always over much too quickly and I would drive home trying to remember what I had heard, and wondering why I felt so heavy. Was it because I had been so free? It was always that way. Neville had that effect on me. I believed him with all my heart and soul. I still do.

Neville Goddard left us October 1, 1972. But where did he go? I can still see his smile (you know, the kind the cat gets when he has swallowed the canary) and hear him say, "Where can I go but within you!" That's where I have found him. He is within me, as he is within you, not as a man of flesh and blood, born to the Goddard family and named Neville, but in our own consciousness.

But perhaps that is not the Neville you want to know about. Perhaps you need to know about the boy who was born on February 19, 1905, the fourth son of a family of nine boys and one girl. I will tell you what I know. You must remember, I am sharing with you my memory image of a man who was my teacher. A man I respected greatly and learned to love, with a love deeper than I knew I was capable of possessing. His name was Neville Goddard.

One March morning in the year 1905, a man climbed the stairs of a wooden frame house on the island of Barbados. He was on his way to see his sister and her new baby boy who had not yet been named. Suddenly he stopped. A voice, speaking loud and clear said, "His name is Neville." Pondering these words, the man continued up the stairs and entered his sister's room. And when he told her what he had heard she said, "Yes, I know. We shall call him Neville."

Living in a family of nine boys, Neville learned at an early age how to share. The saying around the house was, "The first dressed is the best dressed," for if the boys began to argue about who had on who's tie, their father would end the argument by taking the tie and saying,
"The tie is mine. I paid for it. I am willing to share. Learn to do the same." And they did.

The Goddard family was poor in material worth, but rich in love. His mother was a disciplinarian. His father a businessman. Neville used to tell us stories of his youth; about the sand crabs with their hind claws, and the old woman who lived alone on the sand dunes who could read the future. It was she who told one of Neville's brothers that he would be a great businessman, another brother a doctor, but to leave the fourth one alone as he belonged to God.

The fourth one always enjoyed a good laugh. If he had a nickel, he spent it. He used to tell about paying a friend's way into the movie with the promise that he would laugh out loud at the very saddest part. The friend always kept his promise and, therefore never got to see the end of a movie. Or, he would pay a man whose donkey was in heat, to wait at a corner for Neville and his brothers to arrive riding their big jack-drawn cart. I can still see Neville laugh as I write this…and remember.
What I am trying to tell you is that Neville was a human being, just as you are. Just as I am. Yet, in spite of all of his human frailties, Neville was conscious of being God the Father. But I am getting ahead of my story.

When Neville was still very young (in the fifth or sixth grade, I believe) he was to bring his Bible to school and recite a verse from it. Since the family only owned one Bible, and one of his brothers had already taken it to school, Neville arrived without a Bible. When he recited the verse, "Take up thy bed and walk," the teacher corrected him saying the verse read, "Take up thy couch and walk."
And when Neville could not produce his Bible, the teacher made him take off his shirt and pull down his

trousers. Then he beat him unmercifully. Neville was taken out of that school to continue his education elsewhere, completing his high school years at the age of seventeen.

Yet there was a hunger in the young man, a hunger that could not be satisfied on the little island of Barbados. So, at the age of seventeen Neville left home for the mainland, arriving in New York in the year 1921. And there, as a young uneducated boy he began to seek his fortune.

Finding a job as an elevator operator for J.C. Penney Company, Neville worked for $15.00 per week until one day he was told that his services were no longer needed. With a recommendation in hand, Neville secured a job on Macy's shipping dock for $13.00 a week. But this position was short lived as Neville soon became so angry, he said to himself, "From this day forward I will not work for another. I will only work for myself." And that is what he did.

Believing that if others could dance on the stage, he could too, Neville joined an established dancer and began his professional career. It was during this time he married. This union produced a son.

In 1925 Neville and his dancing partner sailed for England and traveled widely in that country. While there he was introduced to the world of psychical research which interested him greatly. Shortly after his return to America in 1926, his interest in mysticism increased as his interest in the theater decreased. And when the depression hit in 1929 and the theaters closed, so did Neville's professional life as a dancer.

During this time Neville became interested in the Rosicrucian Society and met a man who was to influence his life. The man had thought he wanted to become a Catholic priest. While he was studying for the priesthood, his father, a wealthy businessman died and left an estate of thousands of dollars to his son. Quickly changing his mind about the priesthood, the young man proceeded to spend the money as fast as he could.

Having no respect for a man who would spend so lavishly when the country was in such need, Neville found excuses when asked to attend a class the young man had joined. But one day Neville ran out of excuses and attended the class of an eccentric Ethiopian rabbi named Abdullah.

When the class was dismissed, Abdullah came over and, taking Neville's hand said, "Where have you been? You are three months late!" Taken aback Neville asked, "How did you know I was coming?" to which Abdullah replied, "The brothers told me."

With Abdullah, Neville studied the Kabala, a Jewish form of mysticism, and obtained illuminating insights into the books of the Bible. He developed a new approach to the problem of man and his relationship with the pulsating world of spirit around him.

It was Abdullah who taught Neville how to use the law of consciousness and how to see the Bible psychologically. And as Neville began to see the world as a picture world, projected from within, his faith in himself grew.

In February of 1930 Neville began lecturing in New York City. First meeting in a small room of a public building where only a handful of people attended, as his speaking ability grew and he gained confidence in his message, so did his audience.

Neville's first marriage was short lived and he remained a bachelor for several years until one day a young designer sat in his audience. As she listened, she said to herself, "This is the man I am going to marry."

And when they shook hands at the end of the lecture, Neville held her hand and said to himself, "This is the woman I am going to marry," and they did. It was a good marriage. They loved each other deeply, that was obvious, and from this union a daughter was born.

After the war was over, Neville began to travel, holding lectures in various large cities as far west as San Francisco. And then one day he knew it was time to leave New York City. He had hoped to move to San Francisco, as he loved this cosmopolitan city, but this was not to be.

He knew by then that his major work was to be done in Los Angeles so, packing up his wife and child, the Goddard family moved to Los Angeles in 1955. They returned to New York in the fall of 1956, coming back to Los Angeles in 1957.

I am at a loss for dates here, but I do know that during the early years of the 1950's Neville had his own television program. He made two phonograph records during those years which are now available on (Audio CD) cassette tape. He also debated with teams of ministers, priests and rabbis on special television programs.

Neville taught the law of consciousness in Los Angeles at the Fox Wilshire Theater on Sunday mornings to crowds so large the people were standing outside in throngs to hear his words. He also spent several weeks each year in San Francisco.

It was in San Francisco, on July 20, 1959 that Neville awoke to find himself sealed in a tomb. Removing a stone placed there, he came out of his skull just like a child comes out of its mother's womb.

From that moment on Neville's lectures changed. Having awakened from the dream of life, Neville's outlook on the world changed. He knew, as the visions came upon him from that point on, that the garment he wore, and answered to its name, was simply a covering, hiding his true, immortal being who was God the Father. And he tried to tell all those who would listen that they were not the little mask they wore, but a being far greater than they could ever conceive themselves to be.

And from that day forward, until his departure on October 1, 1972, Neville, like Paul, expounded from morning till night, testifying to the kingdom of God and trying to convince all about Jesus, both from the law of Moses and the prophets. And some believed, while others disbelieved."

The Miracle of Imagination - *edited by Margaret Ruth Broome*

EPILOGUE

"I daresay that everyone here would say, 'Yes,' to the statement of Scripture:

'With God, all things are possible.' (Mark 10:27)

I don't think you'd be here if you did not believe in God, and the God to whom all things are possible. But maybe we stop right there, and we separate man from God, and my purpose is to show you that we are not two, that we are One – that God actually became man, that man may become God.
- Neville Goddard - excerpt from 'Live in the End' (19 July 1968)

Thus, begins one of the most profound lectures Neville Goddard ever gave on the imagination, and how dwelling in the end result of our desire will bring it forth into the world of the senses.

Neville spent the best part of his life speaking of the imagination and God as being one and the same in the hope that the truth of these words would be heard and understood, enabling many to live in the love and power that is our birthright. He wrote of visions where he experienced scripture and spoke with authority on the infinite states that the soul passes through before awakening to its true nature… which is God itself.

Although, Neville did not associate his teaching with the New Thought movement or any of the other '-isms' as he liked to call them, he is often grouped into this category. He simply loved to study and talk about the Bible which he described as 'the only book'.

Neville Goddard wanted people to know the love of God and realize that we are rich beyond measure but do not know it. Encouraging people to always choose noble states, was a theme he returned to regularly, stressing that 'you do not have to compromise your integrity for anyone'. He knew instinctively that there would always be those who would make bad choices in life through a mistaken belief that they had few possibilities and would consequently grab at all opportunities even if they were the crumbs that life offered. By teaching that all things are possible and that we can be the masters of our lives rather than letting life master us, he advocated and gave hope of a happier and indeed more honorable way of living.

Neville believed in the symbolic truth of the Bible and did not see the Bible as secular history but as salvation history, literally true and yet happening outside time… an idea hard for our finite intellect to understand. He gave instructions which are as deep as they are practical, concerning how to develop faith in unseen reality, allowing our prayers to be heard and our desires of the heart lived in this world. It is my belief that his teachings on faith are precise, reliable and complete and will eventually lead to purposeful discussion between both Christians and non-Christians who believe that everything originates from consciousness, which is God.

No matter how people's beliefs differ, I hope many are open-minded enough to test these principles out and in doing so, achieve success in bringing their dreams to life.

I also hope it will point you in the direction of more of Neville Goddard's work and lead you to the deeper study that satisfies the soul.
Wishing you great success,

Louise Cowley

Neville Goddard 1905-1972

Salviaextraxts.Com

Made in the USA
Middletown, DE
22 December 2022